1 27 0000696670

SO-AXB-780

Gunnison County Library
307 N. Wisconsin
Gunnison, CO 81230

J
598.9
Swa

Owls

Gunnison County Library
307 N. Wisconsin
Gunnison, CO 81230

Diane Swanson

Gareth Stevens Publishing
MILWAUKEE

For a free color catalog describing Gareth Stevens' list of high-quality books and multimedia programs, call 1-800-542-2595 (USA) or 1-800-461-9120 (Canada). Gareth Stevens Publishing's Fax: (414) 225-0377.
See our catalog, too, on the World Wide Web: http://gsinc.com

The publishers acknowledge the support of the Canada Council for the Arts and the Cultural Services Branch of the Government of British Columbia in making this publication possible.

Library of Congress Cataloging-in-Publication Data

Swanson, Diane, 1944-
   [Welcome to the world of owls]
   Owls / by Diane Swanson.
      p. cm. — (Welcome to the world of animals)
   Originally published: Welcome to the world of owls. North Vancouver, B.C.:
Whitecap Books, © 1997.
   Includes index.
   Summary: Describes the physical characteristics, behaviors, and habitats
of these birds with sharp beaks, sharp claws, and super sharp senses.
   ISBN 0-8368-2215-3 (lib. bdg.)
   1. Owls—Juvenile literature. [1. Owls.] I. Title. II. Series: Swanson, Diane,
1944- Welcome to the world of animals.
   QL696.S8S8   1998
   598.9'7—dc21   98-6597

This North American edition first published in 1998 by
Gareth Stevens Publishing
1555 North RiverCenter Drive, Suite 201
Milwaukee, WI 53212 USA

This U.S. edition © 1998 by Gareth Stevens, Inc. Original edition © 1997 by Diane Swanson.
First published in 1997 by Whitecap Books, Vancouver/Toronto.
Additional end matter © 1998 by Gareth Stevens.

Gareth Stevens series editor: Dorothy L. Gibbs
Editorial assistant: Diane Laska
Cover design: Renee M. Bach

Cover photograph: Joe MacDonald/First Light
Photo credits: Thomas Kitchin/First Light 4, 6, 10, 18; Robert Lankinen/First Light 8; Michio Hoshino/ First Light 12; Victoria Hurst/First Light 14; Brian Milne/First Light 16; Joe MacDonald/First Light 20; Jim Zuckerman/ First Light 22; Darwin Wiggett/First Light 24; Steve Bentsen/First Light 26; Chase Swift/ First Light 28; Jim Brandenburg/First Light 30.

All rights reserved. No part of this book may be reproduced, stored in a retrieval system, or transmitted in any form or by any means, electronic, mechanical, photocopying, recording, or otherwise, without the prior written permission of the copyright holder.

Printed in Mexico

1 2 3 4 5 6 7 8 9 02 01 00 99 98

Contents

World of Difference

The owl is a sharp bird — in many
different ways. It has a sharp, curved beak.
It has sharp, hooked claws, called talons.
It even has super sharp senses.

The owl can hear much better than
most other animals. Feathers hide big ears
on the sides of its head. These ears are so
keen they can hear beetles rustling in the
grass. One ear is slightly higher than the
other, which helps the owl pinpoint sound.

The owl has amazing sight, too. Unlike
most birds, it looks out from eyes in the
front of its head. Seeing with both eyes at
once helps the owl judge how large and

The great gray owl
sees very well, day
or night. Its huge
head makes its large
eyes seem small.

how far away things are. Even at night, the owl sees well. Its eyes take in a lot more light than human eyes.

One thing the owl cannot do is move its eyes very much. When it wants to see from side to side, it must turn its whole head. Its neck, however, is built so well for turning that the owl

Snuggled in its thick coat, the snowy owl stays warm — even on snow.

can see even what is directly behind it.

There are more than 130 different kinds of owls around the world. In North America, there are nearly twenty kinds, and they come in all sizes. The three biggest are the great horned owl, the great gray owl, and the snowy owl.

If any of these owls stood on a piano with its wings spread, the wing tips would reach both ends of the piano. The wings of an elf owl spread only one-fifth that far. The elf owl is the tiniest owl in North America. It weighs less than a bar of soap.

ALL-WEATHER FEATHER COATS

Owls have thick, all-weather coats made of thousands of feathers. Short feathers protect the owl from extreme heat and cold. Long feathers keep out rain. In North America, the snowy owl has the thickest coat. Its feathers cover even its legs and feet.

Owls that fly at night have special coats with fluffy fringes on their flight feathers. These fringes muffle the noise of rushing air so the owls can swoop down on prey without making a sound.

Where in the World

Different owls need different homes. Some owls like dark, damp forests of old trees. Others choose sunny, dry fields or hot, sandy deserts. Some owls live high in the mountains, others in deep canyons or near swamps. Some live inside caves — or even underground. Some owls prefer cities or farms, where they rest on buildings or fenceposts.

Most owls have home territories, or areas, where they hunt. Little owls have little territories; big owls have big ones. A pair of great horned owls might have a territory as big as 5 square miles (13 square

Dark, quiet woods attract the barred owl. It often perches close to a tree trunk.

If they feel safe, barn owls might stay in a barn even when people are working nearby.

kilometers), which is as big as some ranches. When there is plenty of food, owls use smaller territories than usual.

In winter, some owls move to warmer places. They might just move down a mountain, or they might fly to another country. Snowy owls from the Arctic often spend winters in southern Canada or the northern United States. In bitter winters, when food is very scarce, they might fly as far away as Bermuda and India.

Except for Antarctica, every continent on Earth is home to owls of one kind or another. Great horned owls are the most common kind in North America, where they live in many different types of homes. Some kinds of owls, however, need special habitats. Spotted owls, for example, live in old forests. Because many old forests are dying or being destroyed, there are fewer spotted owls now than there used to be.

HAUNTED HOUSE OWLS

It is a dark night. You hear a frightening howl. Suddenly, something white swoops through an empty house and out a broken window. As ghostly as it seems, it is only a barn owl, starting off on a hunt.

The sights and sounds of barn owls spark many stories of ghosts and haunted houses. Barn owls live in dark corners of empty houses, barns, and church towers. They hunt at night, preying mostly on mice that live on farms, in parks, down alleys, and along railroad tracks.

World of the Hunter

When owls hunt, they make good use of their keen senses. They watch carefully for prey. They listen closely. Then they strike.

The small boreal owl uses a low branch in the forest as a lookout perch. When it senses prey, it turns and lowers its head to pinpoint the sound. Then it takes off. Close to its target, it glides smoothly as it brings its feet forward and pounces.

When a great gray owl hears an animal, such as a mouse, moving under the snow, the owl swoops after it. Over the sound, the owl hovers briefly; then it dives, plunging its head into the snow. At the

Hunting to feed its family keeps this snowy owl busy.

13

The northern hawk owl is mostly a daytime hunter. This one has captured a deer mouse for dinner.

same time, its long legs shoot forward to grab the prey with toes and talons.

The needle-sharp talons on an owl's grasping toes are powerful hunting tools. Two toes on each foot point forward, and one points backward. A fourth toe can turn to the front, the side, or the back, depending on how the owl wants to use its feet. Holding two toes forward and two backward helps the owl clutch and carry heavy prey.

Some owls, such as elf owls and northern hawk owls, hunt during the day, but most owls hunt at night.

Usually, big owls eat big prey, and small owls eat small prey. Many owls feed mainly on furry animals, such as mice, rats, moles, squirrels, rabbits — even skunks. They often swallow the smaller animals whole. Owls also eat insects, spiders, frogs, and small birds. In the world of the hunter, owls eat very well.

PELLETS OF PLENTY

GULP! An owl often swallows small prey whole. What it cannot digest, such as teeth, claws, and fur, is stored in its gizzard — part of the owl's stomach. Strong muscles roll the undigested pieces into small balls, called pellets, and the owl coughs up the pellets.

Scientists poke through pellets to learn what owls eat. They might find the skull of a mouse or the leg of a beetle — even the scales of a fish. They compare pellets to see what owls eat in different seasons.

World of Words

Just like people, some owls talk a lot; some talk a little. When owls get angry, however, they all snap their beaks or click their tongues and hiss-s-s-s.

Owls make different sounds for different reasons. They "talk" to claim their territories, warn their enemies, court their mates, and call to other owls. A male barn owl, for example, chants "whee-tuh… whee-tuh… whee-tuh…" to court its mate. A female spotted owl whistles softly whenever she leaves or returns to her nest.

Two barred owls that are perched in separate trees call to each other loudly,

This young short-eared owl is hissing and snapping its beak, trying to scare something that is threatening it.

17

Tufts of head feathers move up and down, forward and backward to help owls, such as this screech owl, "talk."

"HOO-HOO-HOO-HOO-HOO-HOO-HOO-HOO." Barred owls are the chattiest owls in North America. They talk day and night, hooting, squealing, shrieking, whistling, trilling, grumbling — even barking. They are best known, however, for a call that sounds like "Who cooks for you... who cooks for you-all?"

Big owls usually have deeper voices than small owls, but one small owl — the flammulated owl — has a very low-pitched voice. Its voice makes it sound bigger than it really is. Yet, when the flammulated owl is frightened, it meows like a kitten.

Some owls, such as great horned owls and screech owls, have tufts of feathers on the tops of their heads. The tufts look like ears, but they help owls talk — not hear. Standing up and forward, the tufts mean, "Stay out of my territory." Pressed down and back, they say, "Aw, be nice."

HOOTS THAT SPOOK

For centuries, people around the world believed hooting owls brought bad luck. Hunters stopped hunting if an owl on their left side hooted three times. Parents thought their babies would have trouble if an owl hooted when the baby was born.

Some people believed hooting caused sickness, such as tonsillitis. Others thought hoots meant someone would die, and they tried to prevent the death by throwing salt into fire.

19

World of Mates

Many owls have a lifetime mate. They win a mate by courting, and, when owls go courting, they do it with style.

Some kinds of owls take to the skies. The male short-eared owl circles his territory to let the females know he is available. Then he puts on a show. Sometimes he climbs high, hovers in the wind, and sings. Then he glides, claps his wings under his body, and climbs again. For a grand finish, he zooms down, rocking his body from side to side.

The owl also might grab some prey and land. If he has attracted a female, she flies

This screech owl is winging its way home. It nests with its mate in the hollow of a tree.

21

to him. He flutters his wings and offers her dinner.

Some owls depend on their voices for courting. For example, male and female screech owls bond by singing duets. Pairs of great horned owls hoot and bow to each other. When they hoot a long time, they often rub beaks, too.

"Hey, I'm SQUISHED!" These three great horned owl siblings are crowded into a nest built by a hawk.

A male great gray owl hums as he rubs his beak against his mate. He combs her feathers, and she combs his.

Only a few kinds of owls build nests for their eggs. Many owls look for old bird nests, tree holes, or nooks among rocks. Burrowing owls choose underground tunnels. The male prepares the tunnel and sings to a female near the entrance. They might nibble each other's feathers. Then the male hunts for food and gives it to the female. After they eat, the singing, nibbling, and hunting often start all over again.

HOW OWLS WOW

Nesting owls often surprise people. Here are some of the ways:

- Elf owls nest only in holes made by woodpeckers — some in trees, some in cacti.

- When there is plenty of food, snowy owls might lay ten eggs at a time. When food is scarce, they might not lay any.

- Burrowing owls add the droppings of other animals to their underground nests. These droppings make it harder for the owls' enemies to smell them.

23

New World

Young owls take their time growing up; for this reason, some parents, such as great horned owls, start nesting in winter. Their eggs take up to thirty-five days to hatch. All that time, the mother owl keeps the eggs warm with her body and turns them with her beak and feet.

After they hatch, young owls, called owlets, do not open their eyes for days. Their mother stays with them in the nest and keeps them tucked safely beneath her. As the owlets get bigger, she rests close beside them, sometimes hiding them under her wings.

To defend its young, the great horned owl fiercely attacks any intruder.

Father owls catch prey and carry it back to the nest. As hungry as owlets always are, they rarely try to grab each other's food. In fact, the owlets that hatched first sometimes help feed the younger ones.

When owlets grow bigger, they stay alone while both their parents hunt. If enemies, such

If they are not bothered there, barn owls often use the same nest year after year. Barn owls usually live five to eleven years.

as hawks, threaten the nest, the parents zoom back to attack. Owls dive and slash at anything that threatens their young.

Until they are able to fly, owlets hatched in holes, such as elf owlets, stay tucked inside. Owlets hatched in ground nests, such as snowy owlets, pop in and out. Tree-nesters, such as barred owlets, scramble over branches — climbing trees even before they can fly.

By fall, young owls usually are able to find food on their own. Then they are ready to explore the bigger world.

FEATHERED FUN

Owls play with their food before eating it. They shake their prey, tear it, toss it, and pounce on it. Caged owls also play with things they cannot eat, such as wads of paper.

Some owls play with each other. Barn owls play together by pushing and wrestling — owl-style. Like many other animals, they play most when they are young. Playing helps owls exercise and grow strong. It also teaches them to watch closely and react quickly.

Tricky World

Owls are a hoot! They play tricks to escape danger. Some can "disappear" by blending in with their backgrounds. The long-eared owl is especially good at blending in. It presses itself close to a tree trunk that matches its brownish feathers and pushes its feathery "mustache" forward to hide its beak. It closes its eyes sometimes, too. A long-eared owl is very hard to spot, even when you are near it.

Owls also can make themselves look bigger and tougher than they really are. This trick comes in handy when animals threaten them or their nests. To make

The saw-whet owl can hide from bigger owls by blending in with a tree trunk.

When they go underground, young burrowing owls imitate the sound of a rattlesnake to scare away enemies.

themselves look twice as big, owls fluff out their feathers. Spreading their large wings makes them look even bigger. Then, they clack their beaks and hiss to look tough. To look extra tough, they might also sway from side to side.

Some owls, such as snowy and barn owls, use another trick — playing dead.

When owls play dead, their enemies usually leave them alone. Some owls, such as short-eared owls, pretend to be injured, instead of dead, to lead enemies, including people, away from their owlets. When the enemy is far enough from the nest, the owl flies off to safety.

Many owls trick enemies by "throwing" their voices, making their calls seem to come from someplace else. The saw-whet owl, for example, has fooled people into thinking an owl is calling from a tree behind them when it actually is in front of them.

OWLS THAT RATTLE

In their tunnels, burrowing owls make a sound like a rattlesnake shaking its tail. This sound scares skunks and coyotes, which are animals that eat owls. It also scares ground squirrels that might try to move into the tunnel.

When scientists played a tape recording of both real rattlesnakes and burrowing owls in a tunnel, the owl sounds scared a ground squirrel as much as the snake sounds. Its tail hair stood on end, and its teeth chattered. Then, the squirrel ran away.

31

Glossary

bond — (v) to join together with a firm link or tie.

boreal — related to northern areas, especially areas with evergreen forests, such as pine forests.

court — (v) to carry out actions that are meant to attract a mate.

droppings — solid waste matter passed by animals and usually dropped on the ground.

gizzard — part of a bird's stomach with a thick, rough lining of muscle that grinds up food.

habitat — an area with natural living conditions that are just right for particular animals or plants.

hover — to hang in midair over a certain place or object.

keen — very sensitive; alert; quick.

mate — (n) the male or female in a pair of animals that comes together to produce young.

pinpoint — (v) to find the exact place where something is located.

siblings — brothers and sisters.

Index

Gunnison Co
307 N
son, Wisconsin
son, CO 81230